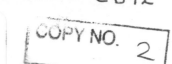

How Ghosts Begin

Clare MacDonald Shaw

How Ghosts Begin

CLARE MacDONALD SHAW

Shoestring Press

In memory
of my mother

 I 4 . 2 . o o .

First Published in Great Britain in 1997 by Shoestring Press
19 Devonshire Avenue, Beeston, Nottingham NG9 1BS.
Telephone: (0115) 925 1827

Printed by Quorn Litho, Loughborough, Leics, LE11 1HH

British Library Cataloguing-in-Publication Data.
A catalogue record for this book is available from the British Library.

ISBN 1 899 549 16 1

EAST
MIDLANDS
ARTS

Shoestring Press gratefully acknowledges financial assistance from
East Midlands Arts.

THE FEET

The new philosopher
at our clinic thought about
my spare feet,

bloody stumps from a dream.
The problem, I said, was storage.
They might be of use in future,

but veins kept shooting up
on the carpet, toes curled
in despair. Try a shrink,

he said. But they'd all gone
bobbing downriver when
the NHS floodgates burst.

Had I tried the lottery clinic,
Art for the Heart? They did a
course on Magritte. Tunnels

and trains. Don't give me that,
I said. Feet, not fetish. I'm being
dreamt, or it's that Jungian

thing. Everyone's waking up
to hear teeth rattling into
the sink. Kids watch granny

coming apart at the seams.
Our new philosophy, he said,
cures this mass delusion; it's

an abstract art, like politics.
Think of the extra feet as
Subject, not Object, being

5

unreal. I let them kick his shins,
but he wouldn't play: madwife
in need of community care.

Either you've sold out, I said,
or you're a fraud. Bet you can't
tell Hegel from Schlegel. Go on,

define epistemology.
He coughed; it's a job.
Did a retraining scheme

when insurance crashed, on
Time and Free Will at Work.
So, was I myself again?

That night I crept out;
dumped the feet on a tip,
left them by a packing-case,

like old boots, airing.
The box began to shake.
It said FROST-FREE

SIX CUBIC FEET CAPACITY.

AMERICAN GOTHIC

Fridges keel over and sail downtown. The store-glass burst at
    32 feet,
though Schrader got the sofas muscled upstairs. All year I've sat
    on his
colonial suites, turned maple or cherry. Kind rooms, open to an
    alien,

your walls are cracking up. WPBZ alarm: there's gasoline on the
    flood,
dying for a cigarette. Silence – breath could ignite – till it's
    drained off.
Small mountains blot themselves back into a wash of sky.

Next day jeep tyres pop, nailed by planks. The unrich flushed out
of timber homes downstream resent us, nosing in with dry papers.
How many people in your house? *Fifteen/No, she's/He's my/*

Shut your mouth. Have you an electric fire? *A what? Where would I
    get*
space heaters? – and the power's off. Dogs nip at mottled ankles,
parked children fight. We dispense milk for babies

in plastic severed breasts, baggy to finger; unstack these horrors
from a greening fridge. Everything's run out, including the pill.
    Last night,
they say, all the heart-tablets in town blew up – nitroglycerine
    bombs;

no deaths, but this is how ghosts begin. Did an absent friend's
    house
survive? Wade over to see. On every sill a radio pioneers . . . *with
    Chlorox.*
Clear gutters, or mosquitoes breed; basements pumped too soon collapse.

People don't collapse; they deal with rats, gnats, chiggers and ticks, sweep
knots of washed-down copperheads off their stairs, tip up deposit boxes
by the Bank and wring their deeds. The air's ripening dead cats in drains,

but the National Guard is boarding stores; the Navy's sending
a cutter upriver with typhoid serum. It's a very civilized disaster. No one
allows this round to Nature; Bibles fanned on the stoops are warping dry.

Her door was a direct hit – padlock on, hinges off. The river went upstairs
in the low foreign quarter. Before hose and broom, grope the sludge for luck,
but tapes and files have cockled, plates stick up like shells. Put out in the sun,

scrubbed armchairs shrink, twang, bust a coiled gut, and go
on the last free plague-cart after all. Water's been making love to her cellar.
Back at the ranch-house I unlock the trunk, a step-in death-trap,

one of those touring vampire coffins propped in the old hotel.
I planned to float off on it when the dam broke. Boring portables
all safe and dry, but the town's lost its past – yearbooks, letters from the dead.

Clots in the blood of time. Move on! there are no whingers here. The Office
of Emergency Preparedness is gearing up for claims. *The Householder should paint*
on a piece of plywood the following: 'Porch Gone: Mr & Mrs John Doe' and place it

in the photograph. Size the damage, including a yardstick or broom, or a man.
All over town hair's being smoothed; the Does are standing like jailbirds with placards,
grave *American Gothic* pairs in front of a clapped-out clapboard house,

waiting for the next life to begin, after the click.

BIRD-CATCHER

Hard to notate – a recital
for sharp zinc pipe, glass whistle,
leaf rim between thumbs.

Icy slides, glissades . . .
the bird skewers blocked ears,
guns down a cat, staccato:

acciaccatura! Steel bullets
melt quickly to brook-water
running over stones.

Undersong ending,
it tries for an echo – each phrase
stretched a note, pitched at the sky.

Più . . . Free-wheeling
of cruel split vowels.
A cuckoo's hiccup,

spring-wound, is tuned
to set keys; this voice rising
queries itself, varies

from quavery trials to rivers
of aria over the trees, and dries
up in the sun;

its lusty mezzo
lapses into a calypso,
rocking back to barcarole.

Luckily for blackbirds
art's the raw stuff of life:
singing either gets you a mate
or pickets a fine green zone;
verse has dried out – papery food
for bookworms down on the lawn.

A gold ring eyes me, song-thief,
dumb intruder. Unpaired, the bird
hides in crochets of shade

a querulous coda.

SEALING WAX

Guano thickens on the lamp,
coral droppings, rock made river
in the sour flame of meths. We hold
stubs to our tin volcano,
building an island.

Her craft is lava. Boils of wax
lanced into veins and leaves
at once turn stone. Umbilical threads
snap from small brooches, mirrors –
our primitive barter, stockpiled

for coasting trade. Back in the war,
house gone, she worked at earrings,
sale or return on emptied shelves; charms
against bombs, necessary vain defiance. Now
she shows me quickhand of wax or paper,

and I make jigsaw rhyme. The kitchen sweats,
condensing spirits from the lamp; forms wait,
sealed in their sticks or coils of tissue.
We open a rose; her scent is burnt treacle,
mine bitter almond, essence of crêpe flowers.

Crusted paste and blisters
deaden the touch. Turning to mineral,
she traps beads on gold hooks with pliers.
Her tiger's eyes have claws. Glass rubies hang
unpicked on the stem; no autumn for stones.

The year of oven-paints I tried out
parrots on ashtrays, wild green birds,
sulphurous, raucous, flat as a page.
I cooked them in pairs; they cracked.
Those days in the quivering tropics

rhyme was easier, rolling beyond
the lagoon. Heatwaves blurred the sight,
yet our mock orchids sold well enough
for the winter passage home. We were
dissemblers, pleasing by artifice,

make-believers. Doubt began in class
where charcoal feet – smudges of bone
and corns – were praised for honesty
above my fervent whirling dervishes.
Fake arabesque; draw what you know.

I know sleight of hand in the dark.
Draining the lamp's purple gin, I
shut art up in its dull room, stopped
twisting guttapercha round wire,
setting words in patterns,

lost power over effigies – molten,
brittle, drawn out of fire – left
for terra firma. She stayed behind,
perfecting unknown species.

THIN AIR

Always at the point of revelation, as the knife hissed
out of its sheath, or the rope became snake (and we saw
it coil through a wicked hole by the bed),

always as the maiden-no-more was about to drown
herself in that effective river, or the arthritic hinge
snarled to a close in the haunted house – the radio died.

Grid bias, perhaps, or the expensive high-tension?
He took out and shook the batteries slowly, his mind
switched to red and black circuits. But craving an end

I'd seize the accumulator – square glass jar – wrench
out its wires, run to the garage. They had a drip-fed
row of them out the back; acid blood for his old box.

Return with the leaking crystal. Minutes to go
before the tangled murder is unravelled. Already
voices are passing silently through the walls.

Ah, but the terminals have to be scraped, he says,
flaking corrosion off their claws. Delicate as
an archaeologist's his hands, thin bone, parchment.

I never found out who, or what, was guilty.
Years later, while I sat by him after a heart attack –
in coma – listening to the ebb of his air,

the quiet radio failed. Avert the omen. Hit
the great box, fretworked into a sunburst, tighten
the screws. Behind me sheets are moving; grandfather

rises. *Man's work . . . not dead yet . . . leave it.*

NOVICE

A body in the bath – it wakes and stares at me
from a quilt. This house is thick with flesh;
armchairs have coupled up in the hallway,
bedding nephews down for the feast.

Jeanne's ironing hangs from prints; old bishops
foxed by flowering damp raise hands, eyes,
in cloth gardens, deploring their chipped gilt.
She pities my cold land, summers without wine.

Madame's at the station, picking up aunts.
Jeanne drags out glass-crates I'm not to touch.
A chef hired with the silver invades her kitchen.
While she counts spoons, he flaunts *bouchées*

all chicken-scented morning. Upstairs stinks
of smoke-bomb; their factory waste breeds flies
in rusty ponds. Pierre lobs dozens at lunch; his dog
eats the dead, out of courtesy, between thrown bones.

Madame returns. Blackest swathes and hat
set off silk wings uncreasing from the Citroën.
Is it the fiancée? *Mais non!* Why did she run out
last night? Will she be back? I'm sent to the terrace,

where Mlle Lamarche sits by laurel tubs
playing patience with the wind; I fetch hearts
and jacks from gravel. Pierre, behind me, closes in.
No cause for alarm, though – married, at least forty.

He shrugs, joins the massing guests. We sit
on iron lace, looking out. She's spent her life here,
distant cousin, loose thread in the fringe; her brother
died young, *là-bas*, down in their factory.

(Was he . . . caught in a machine? One does not ask.)
A taxi! Voices go speeding up; this is the great return.
Photographers shoo us away, reading omens of light.
Blood-kin burst doors, flow down steps, congeal for albums.

Mlle Lamarche will not face the shutter; she is against
all this. Even so, she would have given the bracelet, but
it was taken, it was lost, *mes topazes* . . . Half-told tales –
asides to a foreign schoolgirl – stick in the brain,

splinters from crossing lives. She bares her wrist at me,
showing the mapped palm. We are called to table;
flies skate over gum lakes of aspic, multiply in sauces.
Jeanne has a bowl of insect eyes, black seed-pearl,

sticky eggs; she fishes up for each of us
spoonfuls of emptied sea. On a raft, burning,
losing sight of islands, I shall drift and starve it out.
Or try the caviar, warily.

BLUE FEVER

As centuries end, blue fever strikes. Decadents
caught it last time, from Liberty Japanese;
now dredged-up Nanking at Harrods

inflames collective nerves. Anything cobalt on china
is suddenly more visible, as *House Style*
promotes undustably fragile shrines to sapphire.

(Readers in the grey decade slipping towards the noughts,
be comforted with icons of summer. Catch
sky-melt in our plates, scoop the sea.)

Mud-bed cargoes sell legend: pirates, hurricanes breakers,
the deep sucking. Through reigns, revolutions, fish
gaped at themselves, jellied in ultramarine; salt tea slopped in
                                                        bowls.

In more advanced stages of delirium,
you need a great mantel, baroque,
for the electric dazzle of K'ang-hsi, or Ming mei-p'ing,

and they'll be alien. You understand
a crane, a phoenix, can guess at plum bloom
from cracked-ice Christmas ginger-jars,

but pearls in flames? borders of gongs and fungus?
Looks like a foreign zodiac, needs deciphering.
Our holy symbols – lilies, lambs, Catherine wheels –

flew down to infant heads from Sunday windows.
Virgins, we know, like to wear blue stained glass,
but Chinese scribbles for clouds don't signal fertility.

Later shipments make easier reading.
In sampans, stick-fishers float above pines;
teahouse or temple, the pavilion's familiar,

though English potters have yet to draw
the winning blueprint – lovers, bridge, catkins. Their cups
diluted the rum East to everyone's satisfaction.

More curious, from tombs, not water: rough provincial ware
– peonies burst through compost, cracking glaze – empires ago
sent south to the fringe of Asia, where fever was endemic,

where thin pots sang celestially,
struck in gamelan music, or shielded
the precious parts of the dead – earth to keep earth from earth.

Here, now, the diseased collector
strokes the cold bellies of jars, shivers, recalls
celadon fakes in the shed, the crash in etchings.

Out East, fine vessels, broken, served as pieces for games.

A WASTE OF BREATH

The drinker shields fine wine from an invasive scent.
Palate numb, he scorns a dissolute thirst for oils
pumped from hot wells in flesh, as pores dispense
legal tincture of opium, atomized proof of spirit migrating,
spice-ghost, *spectre de la rose*.

Slow tongues, learning the grammar of taste,
progress from monosyllables of beer, gin, rum,
to fluency in Châteauneuf-du-Pape. Illiterate nostrils
find no primers for scent's dead language –
nouns like otto, attar, root of calamus, and verbs
for smearing necks over the pulse of blood
as incense swung. Passwords to primitive brain
survive: carnation of flesh, narcissus, old narcotic.
Myrrh's that fungal shadow at the heart,
but whose nose can tell styrax from opopanax,
or censor ambergris, floating vomit of whale?

The alchemist has turned designer, setting out phials
among vanishing creams to subvert. He mixes metaphors
of lily and tuberose, translated to aldehyde, adding
chemical similes of musk. Trapped in stoppered glass,
his compounds flaunt their images; odalisques and amazons
spell out bold civet or milk of vanilla.

Dogs, children, fluent in dung and flowers
need no interpreter. Older senses fade with the green wind,
Vent Vert, in a blue hour, preserving dried stems of bouquets:
wine thickened year by year in the hymnbook cupboard,
vinegar air sousing wood and word, or a scarf of chypre
round a mother's neck, faint lilac print on moss.

Scholars teach no art of aromatics;
the good cry rape for lavender plucked and stripped.
Though rosemary oils the brain, and nothing so green as shades
of vetiver will cool the eye, the cynic says, *lilies of the field?*
- *hydroxycitronellal now, a waste of breath*. Do absolutes remain,
quintessences, alcohol for the soul? Exorcise small demons
per fumum, burning cypress with sandalwood; keep to the lit path.
Offer the guest a dry cologne, or vintage frangipani
rich as oloroso. Scent the bitters of life? Prepare for disbelievers;
wormwood in vermouth is easier to swallow.

MONTEVERDI

Coils and loops of music
turn in their shell:
the long-forsaken *ninfa*
agrees with Philomel
that love is hell.

Courteous shepherds, vying
to offer ease,
echo her, *miserella*;
their modulating keys
don't please.

In sympathetic quavers,
fountains weep;
air records her grievance.
Chastened, she sinks to sleep,
numbering sheep.

Pastoral's a fiction;
urban decay
crawls over the meadow –
sister, come away.
Rewind, replay.

QUARRY

Hot quarry, the stink of waste.
Diphtheria down there, says Nan
to crock-hunters, typhoid smeared

on broken saucers, fish-paste lids.
First prize, a sharp triangle of people,
not everlasting rose, bird, rose.

Second, signed greetings from
potters & sons, old partners in clay
and in ETRURIA, BURSLEM.

Elder's out, fermenting
greensick air. The boy rubs spit
off cupids; she says Nan says

germs fur up your throat with pus.
They practise death by glottal stop.
He puts his fractured pink baby

in the shoebox next to its wings,
scraps her pagoda, easy blue junk.
Pollen stifles breath.

Years on, her colds are mortal,
phlegm congeals in septic drains;
sage tea clears it, brewed in Spode.

The dresser's freight – jugs,
sauceboats – is glazedly complete.
She'd let no riveted mandarin,

no half-moon nipped from rim
by time or house-troll
spoil the collection,

but nothing grows in a
china garden. Flung down the tip,
that idle tureen would burst; fission

of painted hearts in nettles, bone shrapnel
piercing sense. Who then might read
fired earth signs, germinal, falling,

inviting to a rococo manganese picnic?
Watteau on Wye; lovers in silver leaf
autumnally flaking.

ANNUAL

Never drawn to life, he watched her
training a rose. High on nitrates,

thin sticks cracked into leaf,
neon came to a head and burst.

His mind was shrubbery; sober privet
spread where bleeding hearts had once

dripped under the Gloire de Dijon. Alone
she fought the leaf-rolling sawfly, cutter-bee,

rust pustule, worm in the bud, while he
read on a striped chair facing the house.

Territorial border-patrols
make suburbs bloom in unison –

double cherry, laburnum. Roses tell
their brilliant perennial lie,

but growths resistant to pruning
sucker in flesh, sap it away.

Her scattered ashes made earth breed
again; bastard stock of sweet-briar

rambled about. Over the fence he saw
oiled bodies on airbeds, burnt to sienna,

cracking apples with their own teeth. House-
bound, the carpet's tendrils writhed in corners.

Winter to come. He felt the gold band slide
knuckle to knuckle over slack skin, foresaw

uncoupling of bones. In the greenhouse,
clearing poisons out, he touched

a leather claw; her mould gripped
at damp. He poured sluggish dregs

into a jar, opened the deck-chair –
cobwebbing rotten, ratchets stuck –

sat in rain, and took his systemic,
cautious, drop by drop.

His double vision: grass greener
than any rose was red. An unfolding.

Air got between packed layers, thin as gold leaf,
and blew them apart; he was yeasty.

Ropes coiled out of knots, dry ponds
turned to fountains, waterfalls,

stones caught fire and melted earth.
Appalled by such excess, he cut

the living daylights out. Flesh crept
down to its sunken garden.

MIDSUMMER

Telling the shrub roses, *hold it*
one more day and you'll get
my full attention, counting up

hundreds of loose pink
cabbages, hybrid musks and
weak-necked purple Bourbons

smelling of cheap soap –
all of them bursting and blown
in the Junes lost to exams

taken or marked, marked,
since I was eleven – *Wait!*
I order the longest day,

but the year's going.
The apple miscarries
an early crop, honesty pods

take slides of darkening cells,
and the blackbird's too fagged
to sing after stuffing its young.

Everything blazes, goes,
and I haven't seen it,
reading these scripts about

high romantic vision,
eyes full of ink. Span
of attention's too short

(someone shaving a lawn,
the ice-van coming) to hold it.
Next life, be ready.